Church Politics

The Mafia: Vol. 1

Nichol Collins

Church Politics

Globe Shakers Publishing Co.

www.globeshakers.com

Online store: Books, T-Shirts, & Prayer pillows

Email via website for Bulk orders

You Tube @nicholcollinsofficial

ISBN 978-1-965553-15-2

Printed in the United States of America

My Other Books
-Amazon search bar type the title and Nichol Collins
-Numerous Children's Books targeting gender roles, body safety, & bible stories
God's Rainbow Promise, God Made Me for a Purpose, I'm Here to Learn, God's Special Gift (Holy Spirit), Not a Secret to Keep, Brave Enough to Tell, Esther, David, Joseph, Rollin' w/ Malik, A Trip on a Ship, Brighter Than the Storm

-Behind Enemy Lines (my autobiography)
-I See Through Muddy Water (Signs of Down Low Men)
-Power: The Benefits of Speaking in Tongues
-Church Politics Vol. 1-4 The Mafia, Greedy Wolves, Strange Fire, Perverse Generation
-Under Construction: Men's LGBT Deliverance Manual
-No Residue: Women's LGBT Deliverance Manual
-Reaching the LGBT: Effective Evangelism
-Walking in Power 30 Day Devotional
-Attributes of Jesus 30 Day Devotional
-The Seek 30 Day Devotional
-Armored Up for Warfare

Yevette Fisher's Books (My Mom)
-Devil Let My Baby Go
-Momma's Last Breath
-What About Conrad
-Holy Toledo
-No One is Exempt
-Walk by Faith Prayer Journal
-In Between Trains

Shall I acquit someone with dishonest scales, with a bag of false weights? Your rich people are violent; your inhabitants are liars and their tongues speak deceitfully.—Micah 6:11-12

For the time is come that judgment must begin at the house of God: and if it first begin at us, what shall the end be of them that obey not the gospel of God?—1 Peter 4:17

God holds His people accountable first before dealing with the world.

Slay utterly old and young, both maids, and little children, and women: but come not near any man upon whom is the mark; and begin at my sanctuary. Then they began at the ancient men which were before the house. —Ezekiel 9:6

God's judgment starts with those in leadership within His house.

Hypocrisy and Corruption in the Church: *Woe unto you, scribes and Pharisees, hypocrites! for ye are like unto whited sepulchres, which indeed appear beautiful outward, but are within full of dead men's bones, and of all uncleanness. Even so ye also outwardly appear righteous unto men, but within ye are full of hypocrisy and iniquity."* —Matthew 23:27-28

Jesus rebuked religious leaders who looked holy outwardly but were corrupt inside.

Having a form of godliness, but denying the power thereof: from such turn away. —2 Timothy 3:5

Many will claim to be godly but will reject true holiness.

Not every one that saith unto me, Lord, Lord, shall enter into the kingdom of heaven; but he that doeth the will of my Father which is in heaven. Many will say to me in that day, Lord, Lord, have we not prophesied in thy name? and in thy name have cast out devils? and in thy name done many wonderful works? And then will I profess unto them, I never knew you: depart from me, ye that work iniquity. —Matthew 7:21-23

Not everyone who claims to serve God truly belongs to Him.

Separation of Wheat and Tares: *Let both grow together until the harvest: and in the time of harvest I will say to the reapers, Gather ye together first the tares, and bind them in bundles to burn them: but gather the wheat into my barn.* —**Matthew 13:24-30**

God will separate the true believers from the false ones.

Wherefore come out from among them, and be ye separate, saith the Lord, and touch not the unclean thing; and I will receive you. —**2 Corinthians 6:17**

God commands His people to separate from falsehood and compromise.

Church Leadership Must Be Accountable: *They profess that they know God; but in works they deny him, being abominable, and disobedient, and unto every good work reprobate."* —**Titus 1:16**

Many claim to follow God but their actions prove otherwise.

Woe be unto the pastors that destroy and scatter the sheep of my pasture! saith the Lord. —**Jeremiah 23:1**

God will deal with corrupt leadership.

I know thy works, and thy labour, and thy patience, and how thou canst not bear them which are evil: and thou hast tried them which say they are apostles, and are not, and hast found them liars. —**Revelation 2:2**

The church must test those who claim to be ministers of God.

Table of Contents

The Truth of the Matter

This book is not a tool for retaliation but an opportunity to inform those who may be naïve or in denial. We are not ignorant of Satan's devices, but we can perish for a lack of knowledge. The goal is to preserve the purity and authenticity of the gospel message and to restore the church to its rightful place as a beacon of light in a world full of confusion and compromise. No one should feel obligated to endure manipulation and spiritual abuse just to prove their loyalty to a church.

It's time for the church to confront the spiritual wickedness within its own walls. We must be willing to call out manipulation, control, and the blacklisting of those who dare to speak the truth. The spirit of cancel culture has no place in the Body of Christ. Instead, we must embrace the spirit of

reconciliation, healing, and restoration. Only then can we truly be the Church God has called us to be—a body united in truth, love, and grace. Addressing unrighteousness compels us to self-examine and repent if we have offended or exploited others.

It becomes difficult to stay the course when so many within the Body of Christ seek to seduce, sabotage, slander, groom, and manipulate vulnerable converts. The focus seems diverted from saving souls, as many seem more interested in building their own kingdoms rather than lifting up the **name of Jesus** and making disciples. It has become a rat race to build followings and go viral.

Cult-like practices have become so common in the church that many no longer recognize them for what they are. However, the remnant is rising with a **holy boldness**, refusing to stay silent. In the early church, those who boldly proclaimed the gospel faced rejection—not just from the world but also from believers who became uncomfortable with its radical transformation.

Likewise today, many stand alone because their voices are muzzled by those who fear the consequences of real change.

Jesus came to set the captives free, and He is still doing that today— breaking chains and calling His people out of bondage!

Satan often works to detour our spiritual walk. Some tactics include:

Temptation – He will try to lead Christians into sin, knowing that sin can create distance between them and God, making it harder to pursue their calling.

Distraction – By keeping believers preoccupied with the busyness of life, he can divert attention from their relationship with God, making it harder to hear His voice or stay focused on His calling.

Discouragement – Satan often targets areas where a believer may feel weakest, like self-worth, leading them to feel inadequate or unable to fulfill God's purposes for their life.

Here's the truth: if you stay focused on the source—God—and **stop idolizing** the vessels He uses, you won't go wrong. I don't care how an actor inspires me through their movies, how a musician touches me through their songs, or how a preacher uplifts me through their sermons. At the end of the day, they are all just people.

Church Mafia

Compromise and worldliness have seeped into the church, dulling its witness and weakening its power. Those who dare to confront spiritual bullies—calling for repentance and a return to biblical truth—often find themselves envied, resisted, and even ostracized. Without flashy platforms or massive followings, they are sidelined and dismissed as "nobodies." Still, these are the very ones who refuse to bow to culture or sell out for fame.

The prophetic voices cannot be silenced. Jeremiah was thrown into a pit, John the Baptist was beheaded, and Jesus Himself was hated without cause. The pattern remains: when truth collides with deception, envy will rise. Envy is evidence that light has exposed darkness. The faithful response is not to retreat into silence but to stand firm in the assignment God has given, knowing that every word declared in obedience will accomplish what He intends.

Over the years, the church has been gravely misrepresented by scandals, financial corruption, profanity in the pulpit, sexual perversion, pedophilia, addiction, and adultery. In a time when headlines are dominated by the moral failures of spiritual leaders, it is more critical than ever to guard our hearts and minds with the Word of God.

As false teaching and manipulation increase, prayer has declined. Many congregations have traded intercession and consecration for personal charisma and outward demonstration. The emphasis has shifted from spiritual depth to performance, leaving believers vulnerable and shallow. Some find themselves connected to churches that have become outright dens of sin. Loyalty to leaders who rule by fear and intimidation creates a toxic bondage that paralyzes the people of God in the pews.

Jesus warned us in Matthew 24:4, **"Take heed that no man deceive you."** His words echo through every generation, reminding us that deception is subtle, and even the most sincere can be led astray. We must never underestimate the potential for anyone—including ourselves—to become entangled in sin.

History proves that power often follows wealth, and together they can become a snare. Money itself is not evil, but it magnifies what already resides in the heart. For some, it fuels integrity and generosity. For others, it awakens hidden flaws, birthing dishonesty, manipulation, and a thirst for control. Wealth offers a false sense of invincibility, but unchecked, it can corrupt both leader and laity alike.

I am not condemning those who have fallen, for I understand that in our flesh dwells nothing good (Romans 7:18). Making a mistake and **living** an ungodly lifestyle are two **different** scenarios. Deliverance and walking in holiness is a **daily decision** to choose spiritual life over death. While some have been restored, others are blatantly living in "gross darkness from the pulpit."

Does Wealth Change People?

View 1: Wealth Magnifies the Heart
Money doesn't necessarily change who a person is; it amplifies what already exists within.

A generous heart with resources often becomes more generous.

A selfish or corrupt heart with resources often becomes more destructive.

"For where your treasure is, there will your heart be also." (Matthew 6:21)

Example — Job
When Job was wealthy, he used his resources to care for the poor, clothe the naked, and defend the fatherless (Job 29:12–16). His wealth magnified his righteousness and compassion.

View 2: Wealth Can Change People
Wealth can also reshape a person's identity, habits, and values in ways previously untested.

It introduces new temptations, circles of influence, and pressures.

It can lead to pride, entitlement, or a shifting sense of identity.

The power that comes with wealth may alter how a person sees themselves and others.

Paul cautioned: *"They that will be rich fall into temptation and a snare..."* (1 Timothy 6:9).

Example — Solomon
Solomon began with wisdom and humility, asking God for discernment rather than riches (1 Kings 3:9–13). Yet as his wealth and influence grew, his heart shifted. Surrounded by luxury and foreign wives, he turned to idolatry (1 Kings 11:4). Wealth didn't just reveal him—it changed him.

A Balanced Truth
Wealth both **reveals** the heart and **reshapes** character. It is like fire: it exposes impurities, but it also transforms the material itself. Some

people harden under it; others melt and become more pliable.

Example — The Rich Young Ruler
Jesus tested the rich young ruler by asking him to sell all and follow Him (Mark 10:21–22). His response revealed that wealth had not only exposed his attachment to possessions but had also changed his priorities—he valued riches over discipleship.

Spiritual Perspective
The Bible warns not because money itself is evil, but because it can tempt people to forget their dependence on God and to elevate material gain above spiritual growth. Wealth, if not managed with humility and wisdom, easily pulls the heart away from faith and obedience.

Many who started well have deviated from holiness due to **unhealthy associations and a lack of intimacy** with the Lord. The **busyness** of life has caused great leaders to grow **lukewarm.** Avoiding the **appearance of evil** and distancing ourselves from those who do not challenge us to live rightly is vital to maintaining a **good reputation.**

Many preachers have taught that speaking about another person is always **gossip,** especially when it comes to exposing wrongdoing. This misguided teaching creates a culture of **silence,** where victims are discouraged from speaking out, leaving their **oppressors** free to continue their **harmful** behavior. The silence imposed by these **false teachings** prevents the **truth** from coming to light, allowing perverted individuals to continue their abuses without **accountability.** Victims, in particular, are conditioned to believe that sharing their stories or speaking the truth is wrong when, in fact, it is the very thing needed for **healing** and justice.

This tactic is often employed by those seeking to protect their own reputations, especially when controversy or scandals begin to surface. Rather than addressing the issue, these individuals will **try to silence** those speaking out, labeling their truth as gossip. We must discern the difference between harmful gossip and **necessary** truth-telling. Victims who speak to one another are often not spreading gossip but seeking **help** and validation. They may be trying to protect others from further harm or even prevent the **cycle** of abuse from continuing. Speaking the truth is not gossip; it's an act of **courage** that can lead to the exposure of **hidden evil** and the **healing** of those who have suffered.

It's not just one denomination—it happens in several churches. The moment you question inappropriate actions or strange teachings, you're labeled an outcast. I have heard ministers inciting violence in sermons, encouraging parishioners to attack those who expose or criticize the leader. This behavior is dangerous and unbiblical, as it goes against the spirit of love, humility, and reconciliation that should characterize the body of Christ. The Bible teaches that we are to love our enemies, pray for those who persecute us, and seek peace rather than retaliation. Leaders should promote an environment of respect, accountability, and open dialogue, not one of intimidation or violence.

Additionally, they often discourage confessions of sin by pressuring individuals **not** to mention others' involvement or wrongdoings. These manipulative tactics are clear red flags. The leader has often engaged in inappropriate relationships with congregants and seeks to silence them from revealing details—especially if the people repent and confide in associate ministers. To maintain control and avoid exposure, the leaders manipulate these individuals through fear, shame, or spiritual intimidation. Rather than allowing true repentance and accountability, they suppress the truth to protect their reputation, creating a **toxic culture** where victims feel isolated and corruption continues unchecked within the church.

Many have adopted a **mafia mentality**—creating an atmosphere where people are afraid to speak up, challenge authority, or hold leaders accountable. This is not just controlling; it is diabolical—a scheme of the enemy to **muzzle truth** and maintain power. It mirrors the world's system but has no place in the Church.

Through subtle brainwashing, people are conditioned to follow leadership without question, often at the expense of righteousness. Fear is not the only weapon—**money is also used as a leash.** Influence, platforms, and positions are tied to financial security. If someone dares to speak truth, they risk being cut off from opportunities, stripped of resources, or blacklisted from ministry circles.

This is why many stay silent in the face of wicked agendas: they are bought into a system where prosperity is prioritized over purity. Like Judas, they trade truth for thirty pieces of silver. Like Balaam, they are enticed to compromise by the promise of reward.

This is one of the reasons I've struggled with the modern church—we pick and choose whom to love and protect while casting others aside, showing blatant favoritism. Accountability is silenced by the fear of financial loss, and the love of money continues to strangle the prophetic voice God intended to keep His house pure.

1 Timothy 6:10 - *"For the love of money is the root of all evil: which while some coveted after, they have erred from the faith, and pierced themselves through with many sorrows."*

The five-fold ministry exists to mature the Body of Christ and uphold the stability of the Lord's Church (Eph. 4). In Black church culture, there's often a **fixation on titles,** with some feeling insignificant unless they're in charge or leading a flock. First, it was the pastors seeking elevation to bishops in the late '90s and early 2000s. Then it shifted to prophet, and now it's apostle or chief apostle. The Bible, however, declares, *"I would rather be a doorkeeper in the house of the Lord than dwell in the tents of the wicked!"* (Psalm 84:10). Every role in the church is vital, and each of us contributes to its function.

Influence often trumps integrity, and charisma outruns character. The office of the bishop, once viewed as a sacred charge, has too often become a political seat. Titles, ordinations, and elevations surge across denominations—many of them fueled by ambition rather than divine appointment.

One of the most controversial and recurring debates in church governance today surrounds who is truly qualified to hold the office of bishop. Can a man be single and still fulfill this role? And what about women—are they scripturally permitted to serve as bishops?

These are not new questions, but in this era of blurred lines between biblical order and denominational politics, they have resurfaced with greater urgency.

Paul's instruction is direct: *"A bishop then must be blameless, the husband of one wife..."* (1 Timothy 3:2). In his day, polygamy was still practiced in certain communities. His command was not mere cultural preference but a safeguard against divided loyalties. A man entangled in multiple marriages— or unstable in his home—would be unfit to steward the household of faith.

Paul presses further: *"For if a man know not how to rule his own house, how shall he take care of the church of God?"* (1 Timothy 3:5). These qualifications were never meant to disqualify believers from salvation or ministry altogether, but to protect the integrity of church leadership.

It is also notable that the bishop's office is not listed among the fivefold ministry gifts (apostle, prophet, evangelist, pastor, teacher). Instead, it is a **governing office**—a role marked by oversight, maturity, and accountability.

Scripture speaks powerfully about the value, influence, and authority of women in the church. Phoebe was a deacon (Romans 16:1), Priscilla helped teach Apollos the way of God more accurately (Acts 18:26), and Junia was 'notable among the apostles' (Romans 16:7). However, none are ever described as bishops or overseers (Greek: *episkopos*). This absence of female bishops in Scripture is a point where I choose to pause and honor the silence of the text. Where the Bible does not speak, we too must pause. God values **function over fame** and divine order over human opinion. Honoring the text requires us to recognize both what Scripture affirms and what it withholds.

The Problem with Manufactured Titles:

One such title lacking biblical precedent is *Suffragan Bishop,* borrowed from Catholic and Anglican traditions. A suffragan is simply a subordinate bishop assisting a diocesan bishop. Yet Paul never referred to such a role. He wrote, *"If a man desires the office of a bishop..."* (1 Timothy 3:1), not "suffragan bishop."

These innovations resemble political ladders more than spiritual callings. They function as career stepping stones, rewarding denominational loyalty and imitating corporate hierarchies. Today, many view the Apostleship as a promotion rather than a mandate. This desperation for importance has turned ministry into a game of musical chairs, where titles are chased instead of truth. In contrast, the early church appointed elders, deacons, and bishops solely on the basis of character, not clout.

Church Politics vs. God's Order

When man-made systems override the Spirit's design, pulpits become platforms for politics rather than mantles of responsibility. Leaders arise who pursue influence instead of integrity, and opportunity instead of obedience.

Yet God is shaking every system that can be shaken—titles, traditions, and thrones of pride—so that what remains is holy and aligned with His Word: *"For the time is come that judgment must begin at the house of God…"* (1 Peter 4:17).

The church must cast off the bondage of religious politics and return to her first love. We must lay aside self-promotion and once again embrace the simplicity, purity, and power of Spirit-led leadership.

In March 2025, controversy ignited after a viral clip surfaced on TMZ. The footage—originally recorded in July 2024—featured a prominent Bishop and gospel singer raising a lavish offering during the 109th Church Convention of a major Apostolic organization. The clip sparked widespread backlash, stirring debates about money, motives, and ministry within the church.

In the video, this notorious figure called on attendees—both in the building and online—to help raise $40,000 by giving $20 each. He supported this petition by declaring, 'This is what God is saying.' In a firm tone, he repeatedly demanded that the ushers close the doors. Rather than a security measure, it seemed more like no one would be dismissed until the goal was met.

The issue isn't whether people should give—it's the **disturbing method** by which they were pressured to do so. The same message could have been conveyed in a respectful manner: "We ask that no one exit as we unite to reach this goal. Please keep the doors closed as we give in worship unto the Lord." Instead, his authoritative **monopolization of power** brought disgrace to the church.

In response, the Overseer of the organization released a formal letter defending the bishop, attempting to clarify the situation. They framed the controversy as a misrepresentation of security protocols and fundraising practices. Rather than upholding biblical integrity, it sought to protect institutional credibility—while overriding the damage done to the gospel's witness. The bishop who went viral later clarified that his intent was to maintain a focused and reverent environment during the offering, not to coerce or detain anyone.

If they as a whole desire to restore trust and credibility, they must rebuke manipulative fundraising tactics, and ensure such behavior is never tolerated again. Anything less is a disservice to the body of Christ.

This is how **cult-like behavior** becomes normalized in religious institutions—when leadership downplays serious concerns. A short clip may not tell the full story, but no amount of additional context can justify coercion disguised as faith. This isn't a misunderstanding, it's about accountability.

Jesus never resorted to gimmicks, theatrics, or psychological manipulation to fund His ministry. The Lord rebuked religious leaders when financial practices corrupted worship (Matthew 21:12-13).

If the reformation is truly committed to **biblical truth**, it must not only examine this bishop's actions but also his **doctrinal alignment** and affiliations.

He has been a member of Kappa Alpha Psi since 2009 (Grand Rapids Alumni). He took over a church and began promoting the sinner's prayer (Romans 10:9) as salvation, which contradicts the Apostolic doctrine the organization upholds. A deacon and his wife I know left his church over this very issue.

A world-renowned bishop, who holds regional oversight within this organization, publicly defended the offering tactic in question, using his influence to sway those who esteem him to dismiss the concerns. This individual, despite his platform, has a troubling track record when it comes to integrity.

I vividly recall, during a season when I had strayed from the Lord, encountering him boarding a yacht in the company of flamboyantly homosexual men. On another occasion, I witnessed him exiting a hotel in the early hours of the morning with a woman. To be clear, these events occurred two decades ago—but the fruit of his life has yet to reflect true holiness since. Some people never develop the character to carry the weight of their gift.

For over 20 years, he maintained a public relationship with a girlfriend before finally marrying her, despite the appearance of impropriety such a long-term, unwed relationship conveyed. Furthermore, he openly endorsed two self-proclaimed prophets from Africa whose practices more closely resembled witchcraft than sound doctrine.

I am not sharing these things to shame, but to expose a consistent pattern: compromising lifestyles among high-ranking leaders are often protected by the system itself. Sin is not rebuked—it is covered, tolerated, or even celebrated—so long as the guilty party holds **influence**. The hierarchy has become a **refuge for scandal** rather than a sanctuary for righteousness.

Group manipulation is a psychological and social phenomenon where leaders or influential figures control a group's thoughts, emotions, and behaviors to serve their own agenda. This is often achieved through tactics like fear, peer pressure, misinformation, and emotional appeals. In religious, political, or social settings, manipulators exploit loyalty, obedience, and group identity to **suppress** individual critical thinking and enforce conformity. The effects can be subtle or extreme, leading people to accept falsehoods, justify unethical actions, or alienate dissenters. Recognizing and resisting group manipulation requires awareness, independent thought, and a commitment to truth over blind allegiance.

Hear me out! Leaders, take heed—what is happening with this bishop's public controversy is not just about one person; it is a **warning** to the entire church. **Stop the gimmicks.** Stop saying, "God said, sow this amount," as if the anointing is for sale. We see this happen far too often on social media. It is a manipulative spirit of mammon, not the Spirit of God.

Let's be real—many Black pastors want to live like entertainers. If you have worked hard and earned your lifestyle through **legitimate** means, that's fine. But what you cannot do is **prostitute** God's people to finance a lavish lifestyle in the **name of** ministry.

Yes, the offering may have been for the organization, but let's talk about the bigger issue. Too many are using the pulpit as a platform for personal gain rather than soul-winning and discipleship.

The time is coming when every leader will have to stand before the judgment seat of Christ and give an account for their deeds (2 Corinthians 5:10). God is exposing and cleansing His church. Let's repent, return to holiness, and lead with integrity—not deception.

Giving is biblical. Applying pressure to give is not.

In 1 Chronicles 29, the people gave **willingly and joyfully**: *"Then the people rejoiced, for that they offered willingly…"* (1 Chronicles 29:9).

Paul affirmed this in 2 Corinthians 9:7 (NIV): *"Each of you should give what you have decided in your heart to give, not reluctantly or under compulsion, for God loves a cheerful giver."*

If a movement relies on **pressure** rather than **principle**, we must ask: **Is it really Spirit-led?** Teaching biblical giving is one thing. **Enforcing it is another.** The **spirit behind this moment** is worth addressing.

This **church mafia mentality** talks down to God's people as if they are mentally impaired. Some defend this shameless display because they are invested in the organization or fans of the **celebrity pastor**.

Had he been unknown, the internet would have universally condemned his actions. Instead, the response was divided—a telling sign of **lukewarm and cult-conditioned** reasoning.

The fruit doesn't mirror Christ's character at all. The Holy Ghost **leads**— He does not **force**. In contrast, the devil drives, manipulates, and coerces.

Guilty, guilty, guilty. This has been coming for a while. The true identity of some leaders has been evident long before now. Don't get a motivational speaker confused with a true man or woman of God. People are often blinded by their admiration of a person's outward representation. Use common sense and insight. Some of the biggest names in ministry are nothing more than spiritual scam artists. Look, listen, and learn, people.

Ephesians 5:11 - *"And have no fellowship with the unfruitful works of darkness, but rather **expose** them."*

We've created **idols** out of people and ministry itself. There are pastors leading churches without the accountability of a spouse, and the spiritual equilibrium of the body is disrupted because the dominant role of men has been emasculated. Hear me out: **I am not saying** that a spouse is a prerequisite to become a pastor. However, in my observation, **kingdom marriage** brings balance and growth in **greater measures** than single men and women shepherds.

Why Unmarried Male Leaders Rarely Reach Megachurch Size

It's not about lacking anointing. Research shows that in ministry and leadership, marriage is often perceived as a mark of credibility and validation. Growing up, it was almost unheard of for a single man to plant a church. Many served as evangelists, but rarely were they ordained to shepherd a flock.

Times have changed, and while it is certainly **not a sin** for a single man to lead the charge God has given him, we cannot ignore that family was God's original design.

"He who finds a wife finds a good thing, and obtains favor from the Lord." — Proverbs 18:22

A wife doesn't just bring companionship—she brings favor, which often translates into the ability to carry vision at a greater scale. You cannot give birth without a woman.

Satan's agenda has always been to discredit the family structure. When men are ribless and uncovered in prayer, they are left more vulnerable. The enemy knows that when the family is fractured, the foundation of leadership is weakened.

This is simply an observation and research I looked into out of curiosity, so I hope no one takes offense.

Public Image & Trust — A wife is viewed as a sign of stability and accountability.

Suspicion of Singleness — Many question a single pastor's sexuality, morality, or maturity.

The Pastor + Wife Model — In many churches, the wife is seen as part of the ministry brand.

Fundraising & Growth — Boards and donors often feel "safer" supporting a family man.

Paul was an apostle and itinerant church planter, not a local pastor. His singleness suited that calling, but the pastoral role carries different expectations.

96% of Protestant pastors are married, and they report higher marital satisfaction than the national average. Having a spouse signals stability and trust. *(Barna Group / Pastor Resources)*

Among prime-age singles in churches, there are **fewer than 50 unmarried men for every 100 unmarried women**. *(Institute for Family Studies)*

In many megachurches, lead pastors serve as **husband-wife senior clergy teams**, making the dynamic a duo by default. *(Hartford Institute)*

This principle isn't limited to ministry. Studies in business, economics, and psychology consistently show patterns where married men often appear more "successful" by worldly measures.

1. Business & Economic Studies

Married men, on average, tend to earn more than single men—sometimes called the *marriage wage premium* (Harvard, Pew Research).

Employers view them as more stable, dependable, and promotable.

A supportive spouse can provide balance, making it easier to take career risks.

2. Psychological & Social Factors

Accountability — Marriage adds a layer of responsibility that motivates men to work harder.

Emotional support — A spouse helps carry stress and encourages perseverance.

Networking benefits — Married couples often expand social and professional circles, opening new doors.

3. Biblical Perspective

> *Proverbs 18:22 — A wife is more than companionship; she is favor from the Lord that unlocks greater capacity and opportunity.*

> *Ecclesiastes 4:9–10 — "Two are better than one... for if they fall, one will lift up his fellow." Partnership multiplies productivity and resilience.*

4. Nuance

It is not an absolute rule. Many single men are highly successful—Elon Musk, Jeff Bezos (before marriage), and Apostle Paul in ministry. Success depends on calling, discipline, and God's purpose. But in general, patterns show that married men often rise faster in leadership because they benefit from the support, credibility, and structure that marriage provides.

Marriage is one of the most critical decisions a pastor will ever make, second only to his call to ministry itself. While a wife can be a true helpmeet, strengthening the work of God, the wrong choice can become a stumbling block that derails an entire assignment. Some women are drawn not by love for the man or reverence for the calling, but by the illusion of influence, recognition, and status. Others are not spiritually grounded at all, but rather sent as subtle instruments of the enemy to weaken the vessel God has chosen.

For this reason, prayerful discernment is vital. A man of God cannot afford to choose based merely on outward beauty or public appeal, seeking only a "trophy wife." The enemy knows the power of unity in marriage, so he strategically plants distractions and counterfeits. A wife called and anointed by God will cover her husband in intercession, walk beside him in humility, and safeguard the work of ministry. Without that, the pulpit may appear strong, but the foundation at home will be fractured — and eventually, what is weak in private will surface in public.

Jude 4 - *"For certain men have crept in unnoticed, who long ago were marked out for this condemnation, ungodly men, who turn the grace of our God into lewdness and deny the only Lord God and our Lord Jesus Christ."*

This verse emphasizes the subtlety and danger of false teachers. Certain men have crept in unnoticed" brings attention to the fact that these individuals infiltrate the church without revealing their true nature. Their deceptive intentions are not immediately apparent, and they may have presented themselves as spiritually advanced, allowing them to slip in undetected.

The phrase **"crept in"** implies that these men entered quietly, perhaps through a hidden or less obvious route, making it difficult for the church to recognize their true motives at first. They gained influence under the guise of being legitimate, often pretending to be pious or knowledgeable, deceiving others about their true character.

The verse further describes them as **"ungodly"** and those who **"turn the grace of our God into lewdness."** This means they misused God's grace as an excuse for immoral behavior, distorting the gospel by teaching that grace permits sinful living without repentance, thereby leading others away from holy conduct.

These men "deny the only Lord God and our Lord Jesus Christ." Their denial isn't just verbal but is reflected in their teachings and actions, which undermine the authority of Christ and His lordship. They led others astray, causing spiritual harm to the community.

The greatest danger posed by these men is that they infiltrated the church unnoticed. They didn't stand out as obvious heretics but slowly gained influence while pretending to be legitimate. This serves as a reminder for the church to remain vigilant in recognizing false teachings, as they often come in subtle forms that are not immediately identifiable.

I will be careful not to get caught up in the cult of personality. Hey, let's be real—some churches and pastors are harming the very people they're supposed to lead. This is what happens when people act as if those in the pulpit are Jesus.

With this mindset, I can appreciate and be inspired by those who uplift me without blindly idolizing them. This keeps me grounded and protects me from devastation if rumors about them turn out to be true. And if the rumors aren't true, no harm done.

The path to glory is not grand and wide but a narrow and challenging road.

Beware of ministries where the focus is all on them—"Look at me, look at me!" This self-centeredness mirrors the pride of Lucifer. Cultures turn into cults when they are not guided by whole individuals. A key aspect of forming a cult is the suppression of personal identity.

Cancel Culture

Cancel culture and **blacklisting** are often used as tools of control in various spaces, including church politics.

Cancel culture refers to collectively rejecting, ostracizing, or silencing someone due to their beliefs, actions, or mistakes—whether real or perceived. In many cases, this happens through public shaming, social media backlash, or exclusion from platforms.

Blacklisting, on the other hand, is a more strategic and silent form of cancellation. It involves secretly or openly marking someone as undesirable, barring them from opportunities, and ensuring they are excluded from ministry circles, speaking engagements, or leadership roles. Unlike cancel culture, which is often loud and public, blacklisting works behind the scenes—limiting a person's influence without direct confrontation.

Charlie Kirk was known for being a media personality (podcasts, public speaking) and the author of several books focused on conservative politics and critiques of liberal academia. He was a strong supporter of conservative causes—outspoken on issues like free speech on campuses, what he saw as liberal bias in education, and anti-"woke" ideology. He promoted Trump and was considered part of the MAGA/populist conservative sphere. He frequently engaged in culture war debates on race, gender, critical race theory, immigration, and more. Some of his statements stirred controversy or criticism, especially from more progressive or centrist commentators.

Charlie Kirk was **shot and killed** on September 10, 2025, while speaking at an event at Utah Valley University in Orem, Utah. The event was part of his "American Comeback Tour." The shooting occurred about 20 minutes into the event; he was hit in the neck.

He was taken to a hospital but later died. He was 31 years old.

I am not engaged in politics at all. I **did not even know of** Charlie Kirk until the reports surfaced—of a public atrocity that occurred in the presence of his wife, his children, and thousands of onlookers. As an intercessor, a spontaneous, overwhelming grief came upon me the following day—September 11, 2025, around 5 PM EST. I burst into tongues, shedding uncontrollable tears. I felt like I was praying for his wife, children and family.

What I cannot comprehend is the reaction of so many. Posts of this man being brutally shot and killed—while his family stood and watched—were met with laughing emojis and mocking comments. A soul has stepped into eternity. A wife is now a widow. Children are now fatherless. Yet thousands found joy in it.

"Because iniquity shall abound, the love of many shall wax cold" (Matthew 24:12).

Jesus told us this day would come and the proof is before our eyes. When a generation can watch someone's life end violently and respond with laughter, hearts have grown dangerously callous.

The Bible warns:

"But I tell you that everyone will have to give account on the day of judgment for every empty word they have spoken" (Matthew 12:36).

That includes mocking emojis, cruel comments, and careless laughter at another's pain.

Proverbs 24:17 warns:

"Do not gloat when your enemy falls; when they stumble, do not let your heart rejoice."

This is exactly what we are witnessing—mockery at death, laughter at suffering, and entertainment in tragedy.

Isaiah 5:20 pronounces judgment: *"Woe to those who call evil good and good evil, who put darkness for light and light for darkness."*

God Himself declares:

"I take no pleasure in the death of the wicked, but rather that they turn from their ways and live" (Ezekiel 33:11).

If God does not rejoice in death, why do we?

Wake up. Your reactions reveal your heart, and your heart reveals your fruit. Even if you disliked Charlie Kirk, he was entitled to his own opinions and beliefs **—none of us should be assassinated for it.**

Some are saying Charlie Kirk is "unalive" because of what he sowed. **Apostle Suzanne M. Howard,** of Integrated Educational Psychology, rightly cautions:

"While actions have consequences, it is not biblical to automatically apply this to a murder victim, as if their death is always a direct result of 'what they sowed.'"

Job's friends made this mistake— assuming tragedy meant Job had sinned:

"Consider now: Who, being innocent, has ever perished? Where were the upright ever destroyed?" (Job 4:7–8)

But God **rebuked** them:

"You have not spoken the truth about me, as my servant Job has" (Job 42:7).

Galatians 6:7 says:

"Do not be deceived: God cannot be mocked. A man reaps what he sows."

This is about spiritual sowing—flesh versus Spirit (Galatians 6:8). If someone constantly indulges in anger, gossip, or pride (seeds of the flesh), they eventually reap brokenness, not necessarily physical death.

There comes a time when silence is no longer an option. That time is **now**.

This is more than politics—this is **spiritual warfare** for the heart and soul of our nation.

The enemy thrives in lies, division, and corruption. But God's Word says:

"Put on the full armor of God, so that you can take your stand against the devil's schemes" (Ephesians 6:11).

We are not called to sit idly by—we are called to rise up in **TRUTH**.

God has placed us here in this moment for a **purpose**. We are the watchmen on the wall. If we remain silent, the blood will be on our hands. But if we stand and sound the alarm, the Lord will fight for us.

"If my people, who are called by my name, will humble themselves and pray and seek my face and turn from their wicked ways, then I will hear from heaven, and I will

forgive their sin and heal their land" (2 Chronicles 7:14).

This is not about fear—it's about **faith**. This is about declaring boldly that this nation belongs to **God Almighty**.

The time for empty words has passed. **Now is the time for courage. Now is the time for action.**

Stand strong. Stand faithful. **Stand together—for God and for family.**

In church politics, these tactics are used to financially monopolize, elevate motivational speakers over gospel preachers, and remove individuals who challenge corruption, false doctrine, or immoral leadership. Those who refuse to conform, expose wrongdoing, or seek true holiness over religious tradition often find themselves canceled or blacklisted—not due to a lack of anointing, but because of their **unwillingness to compromise.**

PASTORS OF CHURCHES: The world is getting darker. Every time there is a service, the baptism pool should be **filled**.

The **new birth of WATER & SPIRIT** is not optional—it is a **biblical mandate**.

When the heart is pricked, that is the moment to **respond**, not weeks or months later. God can fill a soul coming **out of the water**, through the **laying on of hands**, or even through **praise in expectation**.

The Holy Ghost is a promise to all and is given to **anyone who asks** (Luke 11:13).

Too many are told to wait until a class is completed or a designated Sunday arrives. Yet in Scripture, those who gladly received the word were baptized the **same day** (Acts 2:38–41).

We can't allow **man-made delays** to hinder souls from obeying the gospel.

URGENCY is in the land. **NOW** is the time for people to be buried with Christ in baptism and rise to walk in **newness of life** (Romans 6:4).

I have been one of the individuals **ostracized and labeled divisive over the years** simply because I refuse to compromise or water down the message of the gospel. This behavior not only damages the body of Christ but also mirrors the darker practices of manipulation and control—both of which are forms of witchcraft.

Witchcraft, in its essence, is the attempt to manipulate and control others for **personal gain.** This is not limited to occult practices but also includes the subtle and not-so-subtle ways in which power structures within the church can manipulate congregants, leaders, and even entire ministries.

Gatekeepers of Satan: Prophecy has become a tool that keeps many from seeking God for themselves and makes them dependent on the voice of another. The current state of our pulpits reveals a sobering truth: the so-called "gatekeepers" often have personal attachments—whether financial or emotional—to the wolves and false prophets among us. These connections lead them to justify ungodly behaviors and offer these individuals a pass. Over time, these wolves gain influence and eventually become the gatekeepers themselves, turning the congregation into a haven for compromise and spiritual decay.

1 Timothy 3:2: *"Therefore, an overseer must be above reproach..."*

We must approach repentance with sincerity and humility, avoiding a cynical attitude. Repentance is not merely about saying sorry; it requires a genuine renewal of the heart and a determined turning away from sin. Scripture reminds us of Esau, who sought repentance but could not find it, emphasizing the importance of true transformation and submission to God's will.

Scripture says, "*To whom much is given, much is required.*" This is especially true for leaders in ministry—whether an apostle, prophet, bishop, or any other leader. It is dangerous for them to think that living in sin is acceptable as long as they continue to serve the church. There are **consequences** for living in sin.

Another verse speaks of taking communion unworthily, which can lead to premature death. Yet, leaders who waver in integrity often drink condemnation upon themselves.

I would like to share a personal experience that emphasizes the spiritual dangers that can exist within religious environments. Years ago, a leader reached out to me on Facebook, leaving his phone number and asking me to contact him. When I did, he was away from his wife and began to encourage me about my Kingdom assignment. He also gave me a prophetic word about my testimony of deliverance, describing it as profound.

This preacher claimed he would introduce me to influential spiritual figures, stating that my testimony and ministry needed to reach more souls. He asked me to delete a video I uploaded to Facebook exposing a prominent leader's disdain for baptism in Jesus' name. He subtly suggested that I didn't want to close any potential doors, almost like using an underlying blackball tactic.

As the conversation progressed, I expressed that I felt it was best to end the call if he was finished talking. I was cautious about speaking to married men privately due to a negative past experience and wanted to avoid anything similar. When I mentioned this, he asked for details about what had occurred, and his voice took on a sensual tone. Marriage does not eliminate a spirit of lust. It is not simply a change in relationship status, but rather a matter of addressing the deeper issues of the heart and mind.

Although I didn't go into specifics, I began to feel a strange unease, almost as if something had been transferred through the phone. That night, I experienced a disturbing and graphic sexual dream—something completely out of character for me, as I was not engaging in any sexual activities, such as masturbation or pornography, that can open the door for such an attack.

The following night, the experience intensified. I woke up in a panic, convinced that I heard this person speaking sexual things as if he were beside me. It was deeply unsettling.

Seeking clarity and prayer, I spoke with a trusted minister who hosted a weekly prayer line. He informed me that what I experienced was likely astral projection, a practice where individuals can spiritually travel outside of their bodies. At the time, I had no understanding of what this meant, but further research revealed that such practices, often linked to occultism, can involve spiritual intrusions.

Later, a young man shared with me that he had also come into contact with the same preacher. Without offering any details from my experience, I allowed him to vent. He revealed that the pastor had asked him to relocate and serve as his armor bearer, but one of the requirements was to bathe him after preaching, which the young man declined. Biblically, an armor bearer was someone who carried the weapons or armor of a warrior or knight. In modern times, the role has evolved into a person who assists the pastor by carrying their Bible, escorting them to the podium, or handling their luggage during travels. We must be ever so careful—people are doing demonic things under the banner of religion.

Avoid cliques, these lead to cultish behavior—they are not about love, genuine gifting, or loyalty. They are about what you can contribute to build their empire—financially or numerically. This is why we often see the same names on the same events year after year. Once you understand this, you'll realize it's part of a system built on clout and popularity, rather than being **built by God** Himself.

Social media has led us to focus on impressing those who have no real investment in our success or failure. If we're not careful, social media can become a platform for seeking attention, approval, and followers—sometimes at the **cost** of spiritual integrity. In this age of online presence, ministers and church leaders can feel pressured to keep up with trends, which can lead to compromising godly values and principles. Social media has conditioned us to prioritize appearance over character. As a result, living in sin no longer matters to many, as long as it's presented in a favorable light. True victory comes not from worldly success, but from faithfulness to God's Word and His kingdom.

The solution to deception is exposing the deception.

It's not always about praying silently, but about exposing the teaching. It's not just preaching the truth, but highlighting the error and bringing correction. When you love God and what He's called you to do, the enemy will try to fight you. Sometimes, it's not even about you—it's about what you're called to. It can feel toxic and draining, but God is removing the struggle. He will handle every opposition, every closed door, and those with manipulative agendas, naysayers, and critics. God is removing the fight, strain, and struggle from your kingdom mandate. You'll begin to see clearly, and God will reveal who's around you and the intent of their hearts.

Some people heard from God to bring you in, but others persuaded them not to. Discern that spirit—jealousy can hinder God's move. **Oppressors** use their power unjustly to control others. Oppressive behavior uses authority in a burdensome, cruel, or unjust manner. Power corrupts, and when misused, it exploits, takes advantage of, or mistreats others.

Being a disciple of Christ is not for external accolades, but about staying true to the call of God, standing firm in righteousness, and guarding against the deceitful influences that seek to *twist* the truth. Some have traded integrity in their pursuit of **popularity.**

Here are 10 signs your church might be operating as a cult:

1. **Idolizing Leaders:** The leader is elevated to an almost god-like status and is beyond question or accountability.
2. **Fear of Leaving:** Members are told that leaving the church will lead to spiritual ruin, loss of salvation, or divine punishment.

3. **Fear-Based Tactics**: Members are controlled through fear, such as threats of damnation or punishment for questioning authority.

4. **Isolation**: The church discourages outside fellowship with other ministries or believers.

5. **Exclusive Truth Claims**: The belief that their church is the only true church and all others are false or inferior.

6. **Financial Demands:** Constant pressure to give financially, often beyond your means, with promises of blessings or threats of curses if you don't comply.

7. **Hostility:** Questioning leadership, doctrine, or practices is seen as rebellion or sin.

8. **Overemphasis on Works**: Salvation or acceptance is based heavily on works, loyalty, or adherence to strict rules rather than grace or faith

9. **Punitive Discipline**: Public shaming, ostracism, or harsh penalties are used to enforce obedience and conformity.

10. **Groupthink & Conformity**: Members are pressured to think and act in the same way, with little room for individuality or diverse perspectives.

Secret Societies

It is no coincidence that God is peeling back layers of deception, both in the world and in the church. One of the clearest patterns in Scripture is how Satan uses counterfeit systems to oppose God's Kingdom — systems that look powerful, even unified, but are fueled by rebellion and darkness.

The Tower of Babel in Genesis 11 shows how dangerous this spirit becomes when unified. Humanity said, "Let us build ourselves a city and a tower with its top in the heavens, and let us make a name for ourselves" (Genesis 11:4).

Their goal was rebellion. They weren't building a sanctuary of worship; they were building a gateway of defiance. God scattered them and confused their language, cutting off their attempt to erect a building reaching the heavens.

From Babel to Nineveh, cities often became hubs of corruption. This does not mean all cities are evil, but Scripture shows a pattern: where people and power concentrate, sin multiplies when God is not enthroned. That is why cities often attract violence, idolatry, and politics rooted in control. It began in Genesis.

That same spirit of counterfeit power runs through history. One of the clearest modern parallels can be seen in secret societies and ritual-based organizations such as Masons, Eastern Stars, and Greek organizations. The gospel is not hidden. It is open, public, and a light set on a hill (Matthew 5:14–16).

God does not hide His glory.

Whether knowingly or ignorantly, many leaders who entangle themselves in secret societies step under a **counterfeit** light. The Bible warns us plainly: *"For Satan himself masquerades as an angel of light. It is not surprising, then, if his servants also* *masquerade as servants of righteousness"* (2 Corinthians 11:14–15).

Freemasonry presents itself as a system of brotherhood, advancement, and hidden knowledge. Yet at its core, it operates as a false church—a counterfeit altar. Just as Babel sought unity apart from God, Masonry builds its foundation on secrecy rather than submission to Christ.

The **Order of the Eastern Star** presents the same spirit under a feminine form. It appears refined, charitable, and spiritual. Yet its rituals, symbols, and vows mirror Freemasonry. What many perceive as empowerment is in fact entanglement, a counterfeit sisterhood bound by unscriptural oaths. Beneath the surface remains the same false light: it promises revelation but produces bondage. God never designed His daughters to swear allegiance to hidden systems. He called them to holiness, not secrecy.

Psalm 133 shows us how anointing flows down from the head to the body, but deception flows down in the same way. When a pastor or leader operates under a false covering, that deception doesn't stop with him—it trickles down into the congregation. This is why some believers feel spiritually stuck, unable to break cycles: they are sitting under **polluted oil.**

As God continues to expose modern forms of idolatry, one of the clearest reflections of ancient rebellion can be seen in today's **fraternity and sorority** culture. The same spirit that drove Babel's false unity and Nimrod's pride is alive in secret societies that exalt man-made covenants above divine allegiance.

Across generations, Greek-letter organizations have been accepted as symbols of elite status, networking, and lifelong brotherhood or sisterhood. However, what many fail to recognize is the **spiritual bondage** attached to these affiliations. Fraternities and sororities operate under pagan influences, secret oaths, and rituals that are incompatible with biblical Christianity. My aim is to reveal the **hidden idolatry** within these organizations and issue a warning to believers who are unknowingly yoking themselves to **ungodly** covenants. I don't have to be a former member to speak on this. The Word of God gives EVERY believer the authority to confront deception.

This is not an attack. It is a call to examine everything through **the lens of Scripture**, not tradition, emotion, or personal pride. Truth is not determined by popularity or good deeds. Truth is determined by the **Word of God**. Jesus never called us to blend in or keep what feels empowering if it violates His Lordship. He called us to **SURRENDER**.

Hazing: A Gang-Like Ritual of Abuse

Many initiations involve beatings, humiliation, and forced submission through fear—comparable to street-gang initiation tactics. Sororities and fraternities often haze to prove loyalty through physical and psychological abuse. Spiritually, it is wrong because it turns abuse into a covenant test—something God never requires, and something Christ already paid for.

"Do not be conformed to this world, but be transformed by the renewing of your mind." —Romans 12:2

One preacher's daughter came home from spring break unable to sit because her buttocks had been paddled raw. Such abuse is glorified as "tradition," yet it contradicts the love of Jesus Christ.

The Danger of Oaths and Lifelong Pledges

Pledging a fraternity or sorority is a **spiritual contract**. Members bind themselves through lifelong oaths that compete with their **covenant in Christ.**

James 5:12 (ESV) – *"But above all, my brothers, do NOT SWEAR, either by heaven or by earth or by any other OATH, but let your 'YES' be yes and your 'NO' be no, so that you may not fall under condemnation."*

Matthew 5:34–37 – *"Do not take an oath at all... Let what you say be simply 'Yes' or 'No'; anything more than this comes from evil."*

Some organizations even mix **Bible verses** with Greek texts and symbols, creating spiritual **deception.** For example, they have used *Ruth 1:16* in pledging, *"Where you go I will go; your god will be my god."* This is not the God of Scripture, but an idol—a counterfeit covenant.

Don't let anyone capture you with EMPTY philosophies and high-sounding NONSENSE that come from human thinking and from the spiritual powers of this world, rather than from CHRIST."

—Colossians 2:8 (NLT)

Idolatry at the Altar of False Gods

Another bishop who went viral for closing the church doors over a $20 offering popped up on a video reel **repping his frat like a gang,** reciting: "KSI til the day we die. Phi Nu Pi." That should trouble any believer with discernment.

This is not a light issue. The devil is betting on the Church's ignorance of demonic altars. The moment someone takes ritual vows and covenant language tied to another system, they become spiritually entangled.

Many describe initiations where **those pledging** must kneel at a table—yet spiritually, it functions as an altar—covered with symbols, including a patron deity and the organization's name. Some testify they were even required to write their name in AKA's "book of life."

As long as the Greek shield, pillows, and paraphernalia are present in the room, kneeling becomes more than tradition. It becomes bowing in the presence of another god. Whether a person intended worship or not, Yahweh sees it as reverence given to an idol and participation at an unlawful altar. Read Deuteronomy 4:15–24.

Many ex-AKA denouncing testimonies have shared that the Greek god Atlas is literally on the shield, and it is required to be present in the room at every meeting and displayed on all paraphernalia. As long as that Greek idol is present while people are kneeling, it becomes an act of reverence honoring an idol.

Exodus 20:3-5 *"Thou shalt have no other gods before me... Thou shalt <u>not bow down</u> thyself to them, nor serve them."*

Ezekiel 14:3 (ESV) - *Son of man, these men have taken their idols into their hearts, and set the stumbling block of their iniquity before their faces. Should I indeed let myself be consulted by them?"*

Another Christian man shared his testimony of leaving Kappa Alpha Psi voluntarily, in obedience to the Lord. He gave historical context, explaining that the Greeks went to the Delphic Shrine to worship Apollo—who is also the symbolic figure on the Kappa organization's shield.

He said he wrestled with being a "Kappa man" and a "Kingdom man," until the Lord spoke plainly: the tension exists because the two were never meant to be reconciled.

He also explained that in their ritual culture, when the word "Kappa" was spoken, members were trained to bow their heads in honor. That is not neutral. Scripture is clear—reverence crosses into worship because it is a posture of devotion.

God does not share covenant loyalty. You cannot bow in allegiance to one system and claim full loyalty to Christ without spiritual compromise.

The concern is not one's intention. It is the spiritual origin and ritual practice tied to these organizations. People joined in ignorance. Many were young and impressionable. That explains why they joined, but it does not change what they joined. Once truth comes, the believer is accountable to respond.

Sororities and fraternities mirror the number one sin of Israel: **IDOLATRY**.

Boy Scouts, military oaths, and the Pledge of Allegiance are not the same as sorority or fraternity oaths because they are not spiritual covenants rooted in ritual devotion. They are civic or organizational commitments related to duty, citizenship, service, and conduct, and they do not require secret rites, sacred ceremonies, idol symbolism, chants, or lifelong devotion language that mirrors worship. A person can swear in court, serve in the military, or pledge allegiance to a nation without entering a religious altar or binding their identity to spiritual symbolism. "A civic pledge is public duty—ritual pledging is spiritual devotion."

In contrast, sorority and fraternity pledging often involves private rituals, consecrated objects, kneeling postures, secret vows, and mythological symbolism that functions as devotion to another system. Even when members insist their intentions are harmless, Scripture teaches that God weighs covenant, fellowship, and spiritual alignment, not merely intention. The issue is not the word "oath" itself, but what the oath is binding you to.

Civic vows govern behavior; spiritual oaths govern allegiance. That is why Scripture warns believers against unequal yokes and fellowship with darkness, because the danger is not simply membership, but covenant participation with altars and identities that exalt themselves against the Lordship of Jesus Christ.

A person can swear in court and still keep the First Commandment. A courtroom oath is a vow to tell the truth. It is not a vow of worship, spiritual covenant, ritual devotion, or lifelong allegiance to a symbolic "god-system."

The moment they take that oath, they and their children become the sacrifice, granting Satan **legal access** to attack, afflict, and prematurely take lives unless that covenant is renounced and broken. God is sounding the alarm. This is not a small matter. This is **YOUR LIFE**.

"My people are destroyed for lack of knowledge." —Hosea 4:6

"Have no fellowship with the unfruitful works of darkness, but rather reprove them." —Ephesians 5:11

Intentions Don't Cancel Spiritual Origins

Many have said, "Nothing we have done in the secret society is contrary to God's Word."

"BUT THEY DO COMMUNITY SERVICE..."

The Kingdom of God is not judged by positive impact alone. God judges **obedience, separation, and covenant.** Many things can be beneficial socially and still be spiritually unlawful. Scripture never teaches that community service sanctifies an unscriptural yoke.

Unbelievers can do good works too. The standard for believers is **purity of covenant.** What many call "community service," God may view as **SPIRITUAL COMPROMISE** when it is entangled with chants, vows, and symbolism rooted in **PAGAN identities**. The enemy does not need you to consciously bow. He only needs you to **justify allegiance** to anything that exalts itself against the knowledge of Christ.

Scripture declares:

"Casting down imaginations, and every high thing that exalteth itself against

the knowledge of God..."
—2 Corinthians 10:5

The False Power of Secrets & Guiding Spirits

It's not about repeating words. It's about spiritual alignment. God cares about what we're connected to—what we're in covenant with. That is why Jesus said, "No man can serve two masters" (Matthew 6:24).

Sororities and fraternities glorify secrecy, requiring members to take vows and swear oaths to hidden systems of power.

➤ Secret handshakes
➤ Secret passwords
➤ Secret chants and hymns
➤ Secret oaths of loyalty

"For God will bring every deed into judgment, with every SECRET thing, whether good or evil."

—Ecclesiastes 12:14

Some even call themselves "the guiding light." But Jesus declared:

"I am the light of the world." —John 8:12

Why would a Christian take a vow of secrecy in the name of a fraternity or sorority instead of walking in Christ's light?

"Come out from among them, and be separate..." —2 Corinthians 6:17

Financial Bondage to Ungodly Institutions

Members must pay ongoing fees, sustaining organizations that often support unbiblical agendas.

Matthew 6:24 (NLT) - *"You cannot serve both God and money."*

Deuteronomy 10:14 (ESV) - *"Behold, to the Lord your God belong heaven and the heaven of heavens, the earth with all that is in it."*

Christ calls us to steward our resources for His Kingdom—not to financially uphold ungodly institutions.

Unbiblical Creeds & False Religious Systems

Every sorority and fraternity has its creed, essentially a form of *religious belief.* Members must accept and live by it without question.

2 Corinthians 6:14 - *"Be ye not unequally yoked together with unbelievers."*

Creeds in these groups replace devotion to Christ with man-made philosophies. Many join for recognition, power, or career advancement.

1 Peter 5:5-7 - *"God opposes the proud but gives grace to the humble."*

True greatness in God's Kingdom is found in humility—not worldly titles.

1 Corinthians 15:33 - *"Do not be misled: 'Bad company corrupts good character.'"*

Proverbs 13:20 - *"He who walks with the wise grows wise, but a companion of fools suffers harm."*

A Public Example of Spiritual Compromise

Recently, a Grammy-nominated gospel singer and pastor pledged into a fraternity—not in his youth, but in his latter years. Videos circulated of him wearing a dog collar, being led as part of an initiation. To the undiscerning eye, it seemed harmless: just tradition, bonding, and harmless fun.

Why does a shepherd of God's people feel the need to submit to such rituals for acceptance?

At the root of this is a deeper issue: the unquenched thirst for belonging. No matter how many stages he has sung on, no matter how many accolades he has received, there remains a craving for more. But that craving is dangerous when it leads us outside of Christ.

Paul warned in Romans 6:16 (NIV): *"Don't you know that when you offer yourselves to someone as obedient slaves, you are slaves of the one you obey?"*

You become bound by the very thing you yield yourself to. This is why such acts should grieve the church. A shepherd who has preached freedom in Christ is now demonstrating bondage to tradition. A voice that once led people to the altar is now submitting to worldly initiation. No matter the reasoning, be it camaraderie, identity, or validation— the truth remains: when we kneel to anything outside of Christ, we are confessing by our actions that *Jesus is not enough.*

By submitting to this humiliating ritual, this renowned bishop sent a message to the body of Christ that pledging is harmless. But how can a believer exalt the name of Jesus while kneeling before an altar built for another god?

In our latter years, wisdom should lead us to deeper consecration, not deeper compromise. Yet what example does it set when leaders who should be pouring into the next generation are instead bowing to secret initiations and worldly allegiances?

The truth is sobering: if Jesus is not enough, nothing ever will be. If the fellowship of the saints, the bond of spiritual family, and the embrace of lifelong covenant brothers and sisters in Christ do not suffice, then no organization, fraternity, or sorority can fill that void.

Pastoral colleagues, congregations, and decades of ministry associations should be more than enough affirmation. But the wind of trend whispers: *"You need this to belong. You need this to matter."* And tragically, many yield to that wind —even after years of preaching that Christ is all in all.

Paul declared in Galatians 6:14: *"But God forbid that I should glory, save in the cross of our Lord Jesus Christ, by whom the world is crucified unto me, and I unto the world."* The cross is enough. Jesus is enough. When the world sees us bow to rituals for validation, we dilute our testimony and show that the cross is not sufficient in our eyes.

The call is simple yet piercing: in every season of life — whether youth or gray hair — let Christ be enough. Let His cross outshine every collar, every pledge, and every fraternity bond. For if we have Him, we lack nothing. So the question isn't "Why did you join?"

The question is: **Now that you know better, will you obey?**

When people come out of idolatry, the pattern in Scripture is not "just leave quietly." It is to **RENOUNCE it.**

The believers in Acts did not privately "move on." They **PUBLICLY** turned from former covenants and burned the materials tied to them:

Acts 19:18–19 — They confessed, showed their deeds, and burned what was tied to their old spiritual practices.
That wasn't legalism. That was **deliverance.**

Repent, Renounce, Return

Break the spiritual chains and surrender your full loyalty to Jesus Christ alone.

Repent – Acknowledge pride, ungodly oaths, idolatry, hazing, and misplaced devotion. (Romans 12:2; Ezekiel 14:3)

Renounce – Break every oath and pledge in Jesus' name. Declare aloud that you belong fully to Christ. (James 5:12)

Cut Ties – Destroy paraphernalia, clothing, or objects connected to the organization. (Deuteronomy 7:5–6)

Renew Your Mind – Replace worldly philosophies with God's Word. (1 Corinthians 1:19)

A Call to Wake Up

The issue is not whether your pastor is charismatic, popular, or successful. The issue is whether he is consecrated. Jesus said, *"Nor does anyone light a lamp and put it under a basket, but on a lampstand, and it gives light to all who are in the house"* (Matthew 5:15). If your leader thrives in secrecy and hidden oaths, that is not the Spirit of Christ.

We are the light of the world — a city on a hill that cannot be hidden (Matthew 5:14). That is the mark of God's Kingdom. Counterfeit light always hides. True light always shines.

Beloved, do not be deceived. Choose the true "Big G" — the God of heaven and earth — not Gilgamesh, not Nimrod, not counterfeit light disguised as righteousness. Exposure is God's mercy, pulling back the veil so that His people can come out of bondage and walk in truth.

Paul warned in 2 Thessalonians 2:10–12 that those who reject the truth will be given over to a lie. God allows choice. Just as Israel demanded Saul, God allowed them to have the king they wanted, even though He knew it would lead to bondage. In the same way, if people want leaders who align with secret systems instead of the Kingdom, God will let them have what they choose. But there will always be consequences.

Honorariums

There's a common misconception that ministers should speak without charge. On the other hand, some view themselves as superstars and believe they deserve extravagant accommodations and offerings. Let's address this idea. Consider how we willingly pay for services like haircuts, clothing, hairstyles, lash extensions, or even meals at a restaurant—without negotiating or expecting anything for free. Likewise, we wouldn't want to be overcharged for these services.

If you choose to retire and preach freely while traveling the world on your savings, that's admirable. When I am in a financial position to do so, I would love to host free conferences and offer my expertise to the Body of Christ. However, we cannot overlook the reality that ministry comes with costs.

Operating in a form of "false humility" by refusing compensation often leaves ministers struggling to meet their needs.

Ministers, it is not sinful to accept compensation for your time, wisdom, preparation, and consecration. Paul also asks in **1 Corinthians 9:7**, *"Who serves as a soldier at his own expense?"* Ministry, like any profession, involves labor, sacrifice, and dedication.

There are some who demand elaborate honorariums and travel arrangements in exchange for accepting an invitation to preach. This creates a poor reflection of genuine kingdom ambassadors, whose focus should be on spreading the gospel and serving the Body of Christ, not on financial gain. While it's important for ministers to be honored and supported, when financial expectations become the driving force behind ministry, it undermines the purity of the calling. I've heard of some speakers' honorariums starting at $8k for a regular service and $30k+ for a conference. If it isn't voluntarily given, it's unreasonable to demand such amounts—and let's not forget the first-class flights for the entourage.

I believe wholeheartedly that churches should treat their guest speakers fairly. If there is an offering raised for the itinerant minister, it should be given to them without trying to withhold a percentage. The first offering at the beginning is usually for the church, and at the close, some churches raise a second offering for the speaker. In some cases, they don't even receive the full amount. God is not pleased with shady transactions. If a church doesn't have a budget set aside for the speaker, they typically agree that the minister can raise their own offering. What I don't understand is, to prevent dishonesty, why not put the speaker's digital giving options on the screen so they can receive it directly?

Sadly, I have heard preachers transparently share their experiences of being taken advantage of. After big offerings were raised, they were told the check would be mailed or an electronic deposit would be sent after sorting through the collections—but they never received a dime. It's a shame, church culture sometimes involves manipulative tactics that exploit ministers. Phrases like "for the kingdom" or "for the Lord" are often used to justify undervaluing spiritual labor. This is not godly.

Being saved does not mean being gullible either.

There must be a balance between honoring the work of ministry and ensuring fairness in how ministers are treated. Ministry requires wisdom, professionalism, and proper boundaries. I recall, as the guest speaker, having to pay for my own meal afterwards. Ministry protocol requires honoring guests by covering their basic needs, like meals and travel expenses. This reflects the value placed on their time and the important work they're doing for the kingdom.

Before committing to speaking engagements, it's essential to consider the logistics and financial implications. Adequate resources are required for time, travel, materials, and preparation. As the Bible states in **Luke 14:28**, *"For which of you, desiring to build a tower, does not first sit down and count the cost, whether he has enough to complete it?"*

Let me share a personal example. A woman of God in my city reached out to invite me to speak at her event. She initially expressed a noble purpose: to share the gospel with unsaved family and friends—people who might never accept a traditional invitation to church. Her vision resonated with me deeply. I'm passionate about reaching souls and had even been featured on the news during the pandemic when guests on my Facebook Live were filled with the Holy Ghost on camera. I knew this was the type of assignment I could pour into.

Given that she claimed her church wasn't backing the event financially, I agreed to minister for a small token of love. I respected her transparency—or so I thought.

Later, however, she revealed they wanted to "avoid anything churchy." That revelation made me pause. I began to question the true intentions of the event. *Do you want to win souls—or do you just want to entertain?* I wondered.

As the main speaker, I naturally assumed my mother's ticket for the Mother's Day luncheon would be complimentary. When I inquired, however, I was told it had only been reduced to half-price. I couldn't help but feel slighted—especially after the host shared with me her excitement about covering flights and hotel accommodations for two strangers who weren't even on the program. She had recently connected with a grieving mother on Facebook who had lost a child and requested that her daughter be flown out with her. While I truly sympathized with her pain, the inconsistency was evident.

I lived locally, so I wasn't costing her anything in travel or accommodations. Yet I was asked to adjust to a "tight budget" while others—who had no role in the program—were being flown in and housed. The situation felt disingenuous. How could she claim financial strain while simultaneously allocating resources elsewhere? For me, it was never about the money—it was about principle, stewardship, and the clear misalignment between her words and her actions. When I respectfully raised the concern, she turned it back on me, accusing me of operating in a spirit of greed.

I replied, "If I were greedy, I would have declined your invitation from the beginning. The few hundred dollars you offered will barely cover the expense of purchasing an outfit in the color scheme required for speakers, along with my hair appointment. I am practically walking away with nothing. That does not reflect greed—I accepted a minimal love offering because you said your funds were limited. Yet at the same time, you are investing in custom-made seat covers instead of reusing last year's decorations, and flying in strangers who were on nationwide news after the tragic loss of a son. I discern that your motive is to project a certain image before your church peers."

She twisted the scenario. She painted me as someone trying to **hustle** her. She even said I was "reverting back to the street." I was stunned—not just by the manipulation, but by the **dishonor**.

In the end, I canceled altogether. I couldn't, in good conscience, continue with so much confusion and lack of spiritual integrity.

This experience taught me something critical: **Value your time, effort, and anointing.**

If someone's only motive for ministry is **financial gain**, they are *peddling the Word of God*—exactly what Paul warned against:

2 Corinthians 2:17 - *"Unlike so many, we do not peddle the word of God for profit. On the contrary, in Christ we speak before God with sincerity, as those sent from God."*

At the same time, **fair compensation** for spiritual labor **aligns with Scripture**.

Souls are the goal, but ministers are worthy of **honor and support**.

Ministry requires intentionality, prayer, and stewardship. Don't waste your time, your resources, or your **oil** on engagements where your calling is undervalued.

People will pay **thousands** to bring in popular names or gospel artists—yet expect sincere, lesser-known ministers to **leave wondering how their bills will be paid**.

Still, how much more valuable is **spiritual nourishment?** The apostle Paul offers wisdom on this matter:

1 Corinthians 9:11 – *"If we have sown spiritual things among you, is it too much if we reap material things from you?"*

1 Corinthians 9:14 – *"In the same way, the Lord commanded that those who proclaim the gospel should get their living by the gospel."*

1 Timothy 5:17–18 – *"The elders who direct the affairs of the church well are worthy of double honor, especially those whose work is preaching and teaching. For Scripture says, 'Do not muzzle an ox while it is treading out the grain,' and, 'The worker deserves his wages.'"*

On a broader scale, I've noticed a troubling pattern. Churches and conference hosts often prioritize **big names** and **social clout** over seeking God's direction. I'm not saying that well-known preachers aren't called, many of them truly are. But too often, people claim, *"God told us to bring in so-and-so,"* when in reality, it's simply about **filling seats** and **raising offerings**.

It's marketing masquerading as ministry and fundraising clothed in false prophecy.

Let your yes be yes and your no be no. Value your assignment, protect your anointing, and **never allow someone else's manipulation to silence your discernment**. We are not for sale. We are sent.

The Racial Divide

The church cannot effectively move forward without acknowledging where we came from. History matters because it reveals the patterns we often repeat. If we don't understand how we got here, we will continue to walk in cycles of division, even in the name of revival.

The Azusa Street Revival of 1906 marked a rare moment when the Holy Spirit moved with such power that racial and social divisions were pushed aside. Under the leadership of a Black man, William J. Seymour, men and women of all races came together, speaking in tongues, laying hands on the sick, and experiencing the outpouring of the Holy Ghost. For a brief moment, race didn't matter—only being filled with the Spirit.

But what happened when the revival ended? When people left California and returned to their respective cities, the racial unity they had experienced at Azusa didn't last. Many reverted to the segregationist mindset of the time, leading to the eventual racial split in Pentecostalism.

The PAW Split and the Formation of the UPCI

One of the most significant racial divisions in Pentecostal history was the split within the Pentecostal Assemblies of the World (PAW). Originally, the PAW was an interracial organization. However, due to racial tensions and the pressures of segregation in the 1920s, white ministers began to separate themselves from Black leadership.

By 1945, this division led to the formation of the United Pentecostal Church International (UPCI)—a merger of two predominantly white Oneness Pentecostal groups: the Pentecostal Church, Incorporated (PCI) and the Pentecostal Assemblies of Jesus Christ (PAJC). The PAW, which had once been interracial, became a predominantly Black organization, while the UPCI remained largely white. This division wasn't about doctrine—it was about race. The leadership of the time reflected the societal norms of segregation, proving that even revival could not completely break the chains of racism in the church.

Why Representation Matters

If you want to know how much an organization values the voice of an African American, look at its top leadership. If we are not represented in the first four key leadership positions, that is a sign that our voices are not truly being considered. Tokenism is not representation. Having a few Black leaders in minor roles while keeping major decisions in the hands of a white majority is not progress—it's pacification.

This is why proper representation in leadership is critical. The racial split of Pentecostalism wasn't just a historical event—it is a pattern that continues today. Many organizations still struggle with diversity in their leadership, and until these structures are changed, we cannot claim to be a truly unified church.

The Azusa revival gave us a glimpse of what true unity in the Spirit looks like. But unity requires more than just a temporary experience—it requires intentional change. It is not enough to invite Black voices into the room; they must be given authority at the table.

If we are serious about revival, we must be serious about representation. We must ask hard questions:

· Are Black leaders given true decision-making power, or are they just there for show?

· Are organizations willing to break historic racial strongholds in their structure, or are they comfortable maintaining the status quo?

· Are we moving toward real unity, or are we just repeating history in a different form?

Until the church fully embraces what Azusa was meant to be—a movement where race does not determine position, authority, or calling—we will continue to see division masquerading as unity. It's time to move forward, but we cannot do so without first acknowledging where we've been.

For decades, white Pentecostal circles have misused scripture to impose unnecessary cultural customs on believers, creating **division** rather than unity. These traditions, often presented as biblical mandates, have been used to **control and suppress**, particularly targeting Black Christians. Instead of embracing the diversity within the body of Christ, many churches have **weaponized selective legalism** to uphold cultural biases, making Black believers feel unwelcome or inferior simply for expressing their faith or presentation differently.

It's no secret that some white Pentecostal churches hold Black Christians to a different standard. While they claim holiness is about the heart, their actions suggest otherwise. They dismiss vibrant forms of worship, criticize outward appearances, and judge our appearance based on their own **man-made** traditions. This double standard creates an environment where Black believers are viewed as carnal if a woman wears pants or a man wears facial hair. Ironically, they would rather see men completely shaven—

resembling a **Ru Paul's Drag Race** contestant—than allow them to embrace natural masculinity. **If Jesus' beard was plucked out at Calvary what is the problem?**

Pants did not even exist when Deuteronomy 22:5 was written. Both men and women wore tunics, and the commandment was addressing something entirely different. Historically, men would shave their faces to pass as women during wartime, and appearing as the opposite gender was linked to pagan worship of false gods. Yet, instead of understanding the **historical and cultural context,** some have twisted this scripture to push their own legalistic agenda.

I experienced this firsthand at a United Pentecostal Church in Toledo, Ohio, where my mother and I were deliberately avoided as visitors. Unlike the warm, welcoming atmosphere a church should have, we were met with cold indifference. The pastor made himself appear busy after service, avoiding us completely as we waited patiently to meet him. It became clear that we **didn't fit the mold** of their version of "holiness."

The congregation itself looked like a a group of pilgrims—women all in uniform, wearing either tight, high buns or long, stringy, untrimmed hair. It is taught that even cutting off split ends for basic hair health is considered sinful. Meanwhile, the men freely praised God, while the women stood in silent compliance, as if their voices or praise were forbidden. My mother and I, in contrast, had our hair styled with a touch of highlight, and that alone was enough to brand us as outsiders. We were not seen as holy—because in their eyes, holiness was about **conformity,** not a heart transformation.

The irony is that many of these rules stem from traditions that were never biblical in the first place. Scripture has been **manipulated to bind believers** to outdated customs that **do not define** righteousness. Meanwhile, real issues—like **racial bias, classism, and favoritism**—are ignored. These same leaders who condemn outward appearances have no problem upholding systems that exclude, oppress, and control.

This **prejudiced mindset** has led to an unspoken hierarchy within church culture. White believers are often given more grace, more opportunities, and more acceptance, while Black believers are **scrutinized** for everything from their style of dress to their expressions of faith. We are told to tone down, to assimilate, or to prove our holiness in ways that have **nothing** to do with the heart. Once we speak out against these injustices, we are labeled as rebellious or divisive.

The truth is, real division comes from the refusal to acknowledge and correct these prejudiced behaviors. True **unity** in the body of Christ is not about forcing conformity to one cultural standard—it's about embracing the uniqueness God has placed in each of us. It's time to call out these **strongholds and break free from religious systems** that prioritize personal preferences over biblical truth. The kingdom of God is not built on racial superiority or man-made customs—it is built on **Christ alone.**

The Spirit of Imitation

Imitation is never the real thing. It may look similar on the outside, but it will always lack the depth, substance, and authenticity of the original. Think about imitation products we see every day— like imitation crab meat. It's packaged to resemble the real thing, and it may even be seasoned to taste somewhat like it, but it is still a processed substitute. No matter how convincing it appears, it can never carry the same value or essence as genuine crab.

In the same way, people can imitate in the spiritual realm. They mirror the look, the sound, and even the story of another person's life, but it remains surface-level duplication. They cannot reproduce what God Himself has authored through the fire of personal experience. Many who come out of LGBT backgrounds focus on dressing up a spirit and rushing into marriage, yet still secretly desire the same sex— lacking the true ONENESS that comes only through genuine deliverance.

I saw this reality unfold through a female minister I will call Paulette. She was fervent in her exhortations on social media, and early on I sensed she may have shared a background similar to mine. I gathered this from her mannerisms and presentation, though she never directly stated it. Even so, she appeared sincere in her walk with God, and because I was still walking through my own process of deliverance, I did not rush to judgment.

At the time, my hair was still growing out, so I wore wigs to present a more feminine appearance. Paulette wore a short Mohawk style. I was in a season of deep fasting and prayer, seeking freedom from strongholds that had held me captive for twenty years. During that period, I began sharing scriptures and prayers online, grateful to see others with similar backgrounds standing for the Lord.

One evening, I felt led to share my testimony on Periscope. I was nervous, so before going live, I prayed in tongues for nearly an hour to build courage. When I finally shared what God was doing in my life, the response was overwhelming. Viewers offered encouragement, and I uploaded the replay to Facebook for others to watch.

Paulette and I were already connected on social media, and about twenty minutes after I posted the link, she commented about how powerful my testimony was. That made me pause, and I wondered how she had been able to watch so quickly. Perhaps she skimmed through the video or had been viewing silently during the live.

The very next day, she went online to share her own testimony of being delivered from a lesbian lifestyle. I tuned in and offered encouragement in the comments. Still, I found it surprising when she mentioned it had been almost ten years since she had been involved in same-sex relationships. Her style of dress and mannerisms were still masculine. Then, I wondered why she was only now choosing to share her story publicly.

She spoke about a career path that did not work out and how God called her into ministry. She also described being saved alongside her mother, which was a beautiful testimony.

As time passed, I began noticing what felt like a pattern. When I posted a testimony photo, she would post one the same day. After I wore a burgundy wig, she dyed her Mohawk burgundy. I did a Periscope broadcast from my balcony, and the same week she broadcast from hers. I hosted a cooking show making tacos, and she did a cooking show making tacos as well.

Things intensified when I announced I was writing my autobiography. Within the same month, she released a book of her own. After I styled my hair professionally to celebrate my book release, she later appeared with a similar hairstyle on the cover of another project. She also used the phrase "Caterpillar to Butterfly," which held personal meaning in my testimony, even though she had previously used a different slogan, "Athlete to Anointed." My book title was designed in camouflage lettering, which later became part of my clothing theme, and in time she adopted camouflage styling as well. At times, her actions felt strategic and competitive, and her platform grew through larger ministry endorsements.

The most difficult moment came when we were both featured on the same television network. As she shared her testimony, I began hearing details that closely resembled parts of my life story. I remembered earlier broadcasts where her narrative sounded different, which left me confused as to how certain elements had developed over time.

I also remembered a previous Periscope testimony where she had spoken about concerns regarding her mother's smoking habit. Later, on television, she described her mother as someone who had prayed her out of homosexuality — a theme deeply connected to my own mother's story, which had been publicly documented in her book *Devil Let My Baby Go*. She also began sharing additional elements about her past — including abuse, wearing women's apparel for the first time on Mother's Day, and gang affiliations — things I had not previously heard her mention, yet which closely paralleled aspects of my own testimony.

It was deeply unsettling. I found myself asking, who repeats another person's testimony in such similar detail? To me, it felt manufactured, as though pieces of stories were being assembled for emotional impact. Over time, it became painfully clear to me that experiences I had lived through seemed to be hijacked in another narrative. What God gave me as a testimony of His power felt mirrored in ways that were difficult to process. No outward appearance or adopted narrative can substitute for true deliverance. Sadly, church politics and competition sometimes show up in places they should never exist.

At times, the situation felt surreal, almost like a performance built on overlapping details rather than distinct journeys. Yet through it all, God taught me something invaluable: imitation may persuade for a season, but it can never carry the weight of authenticity. What is birthed in prayer, fasting, and tears cannot be reproduced through comparison or competition. That is the dividing line between the genuine and the imitation.

That realization forced me into prayer, reflection, and ultimately forgiveness. I had to confront the fact that offense had taken root in my heart, and I needed deliverance from that. Testimonies are sacred, and what God did in my life was real. No imitation could erase what heaven recorded.

I made a choice to remain in my anointed lane, comforted by God Himself as the defender of truth. My responsibility is to walk in deliverance, stay healed, and stay faithful to the assignment He gave me.

CATERPILLAR 2 BUTTERFLY

Me   Paulette

Kingdom Co-Dependency

Some people in ministry don't just serve out of love for God—they serve to feel needed, validated, or seen by church leadership. Their identity becomes wrapped up in being *the one everyone calls*, *the one who fixes things*, *the one who never says no*. Sacrifice becomes their love language, but not unto the Lord—unto **people**.

Sadly, many leaders feed off this cycle. Instead of **honoring** the hearts of those who serve, they drain them **dry**. They become spiritual leeches—pulling from the loyalty, availability, and gifts of others without ever pouring back. For them, ministry isn't about nurturing souls; it's about keeping power, control, and a constant supply of people who will *do the work* while they **reap** the benefits.

And what happens? The servant feels trapped—needed but never truly valued. Constantly pouring out, constantly exhausted, but afraid to stop because *being needed* became their identity. They confuse abuse for assignment, thinking that enduring mistreatment is part of their calling.

Codependency in ministry is deeper than generosity or being helpful. It's when your sense of worth is tied to how *useful* you are to people—especially leadership. You feel important when you're the fixer, the rescuer, the dependable one—even when the people you serve don't honor or respect you.

It looks like:

Saying yes when your spirit is screaming no.

Feeling guilty for resting because you might *let someone down.*

Believing you're closer to God because you suffer silently.

Pouring yourself out while your leaders (and others) keep taking, never checking if you're okay.

At its root, it's not ministry—it's **bondage** disguised as servanthood. And it feeds both the codependent *and* the manipulative leader who thrives off your sacrifice.

God never intended for your identity to be rooted in how much you can *do* or how many problems you can *solve* for others. Your purpose is not to carry the weight of a ministry while others sit back and watch you burn out. True fulfillment is found in Him—not in titles, positions, or applause from leadership.

Shifting from People-Pleasing to Purpose-Fulfilling

1. Recognize the Cycle

Ask yourself: *Am I serving God or trying to stay needed by people?* If you're honest, some of the things you call "serving" are actually fear of losing your place or favor with leadership.

2. Set Boundaries Without Apology

Even Jesus withdrew from the crowds to rest and pray (Luke 5:16). You are allowed to say, *"I can't today."* Burning out doesn't make you more spiritual.

3. Know Your Worth in Christ

God doesn't love you more because you stayed late or took on extra work. He loves you because you're His child. Period.

4. Refuse to be Manipulated by Guilt

Some leaders know exactly what they're doing when they guilt-trip you into saying yes. Learn to recognize emotional and spiritual manipulation. You are not called to be someone's crutch.

5. Pursue Healthy, Mutual Relationships

Godly leadership honors, uplifts, and respects those who serve—not just uses them. If you're always pouring and never being poured into, something is out of order.

Kindness, loyalty, and a servant's heart are beautiful—but when they become tools for manipulation, it's no longer ministry it's **spiritual abuse**. God wants you to serve from *strength*, not *survival mode.* You are more than your position, more than your sacrifice, and *more than what you do for other people.*

If you've found yourself stuck in this cycle—overextending, burned out, chasing validation—it's time to break free.

You are enough even when you're not needed. You are loved, valued, and complete in Him.

Serve God, not man. Love people, but don't lose yourself trying to prove your worth. The only *well done* that truly matters will come from the Lord—not a title, not a leader, not a pulpit.

A Tumultuous Marriage

Marriage is designed by God to be a covenant of love, safety, and mutual honor. Scripture declares that husbands are to love their wives *"as Christ loved the church and gave Himself for it"* (Ephesians 5:25). This is not merely a poetic command, it is the divine standard. Anything less than love, respect, and sacrificial care is a distortion of God's intention for marriage. Yet, too often within the church, tumultuous marriages—filled with verbal abuse, emotional neglect, and even physical violence—have been swept under the rug in the name of "preserving the covenant."

When Silence Becomes Complicity

Tragically, there are countless testimonies of women and men who have been counseled by church leaders to remain in abusive relationships.

Some have even been warned against calling the police, as though involving the authorities somehow dishonors God. Others have been told to endure abuse "for the sake of the children" or to keep up appearances in the congregation. These responses, though often cloaked in piety, can amount to spiritual negligence. When the church chooses silence, it becomes complicit in the destruction of lives.

The Scriptures never sanction abuse. On the contrary, Jesus came to bring liberty to the oppressed (Luke 4:18). When the church discourages victims from seeking safety and justice, it is not preserving marriage—it is perpetuating bondage. We must be careful never to equate suffering under sin with carrying a cross. Christ's cross was redemptive; an abusive marriage is destructive.

What About "God Hates Divorce"?

One of the most misapplied verses is *"God hates divorce"* (Malachi 2:16). This passage is often quoted as if it were the final word on every marriage, regardless of the circumstances. But we must read it in context: God was rebuking men who treacherously abandoned their wives without cause, breaking covenant for selfish reasons. He was not commanding victims to stay bound to abuse.

Consider the woman who came to her pastor with tears in her eyes, confessing that her husband's rages had turned violent. Instead of offering protection or calling the authorities, she was told, *"God hates divorce. Just pray harder. Submit more. God will change him."* That counsel not only dismissed her suffering but endangered her very life.

Or the man whose wife continually belittled him, drained the family finances, and openly flaunted adulterous relationships. When he sought counsel, he was told, *"Stay quiet for the children's sake. A divorce will ruin your ministry."* Here, "God hates divorce" was weaponized to silence someone who desperately needed biblical wisdom and support.

Yes, divorce grieves God—because it represents the breaking of covenant and the pain of separation. **Abuse, betrayal, and abandonment grieve Him as well.** Scripture recognizes grounds for release: Jesus acknowledged adultery as a cause (Matthew 19:9).

God's heart is never to see His children crushed under violence and torment. It is also vital to remember that while God hates divorce, the **only unforgivable sin in Scripture is blasphemy against the Holy Spirit** (Mark 3:28–29). Divorce, though painful and serious, is not beyond God's forgiveness. When we elevate divorce as though it were the unpardonable sin, we misrepresent the gospel. The blood of Jesus cleanses from *all* unrighteousness (1 John 1:9).

The Misuse of "Sanctified by the Wife"

Another verse that is often twisted is *"the unbelieving husband is sanctified by the wife"* (1 Corinthians 7:14). Some churches have used this passage to pressure women into staying in marriages where they are carrying the entire spiritual burden of the household.

However, Paul's teaching here was not a command to remain in abusive situations, nor a call for one spouse to play Savior.

The Greek word translated "sanctified" is ἡγίασται *(hēgiastai)*, which means "set apart" or "consecrated for a special purpose." Paul was teaching that the presence of a believing spouse sets the home apart under a measure of God's covering and influence. This sanctification is not salvation—it does not mean the unbelieving spouse is automatically saved. It simply means the marriage and household benefit from the godly influence of the believer.

This was never meant to imply that a woman must suffer endlessly in the hope that her faith alone will transform an unrepentant partner. Nor does it mean a man must silently endure a destructive marriage while being told, *"your prayers will sanctify her."* A spouse is not called to carry the entire load of redemption for their family—Christ alone bears that weight.

When this verse is misapplied, it places an unbearable yoke on believers, making them martyrs for dysfunction instead of vessels of God's peace. The intent was to highlight God's grace in households where faith and unbelief coexist, not to trap anyone in cycles of abuse or oppression.

With the Greek nuance included, you're showing clearly:

Sanctified = set apart, under influence, not saved.

Paul was encouraging balance, not bondage.

Christ is the redeemer, not the spouse.

The Toll of Verbal and Emotional Abuse

Verbal abuse, though less visible than physical harm, takes a profound toll on the mind and spirit. Constant belittling, shouting, manipulation, and threats corrode a person's self-worth and can lead to depression, anxiety, and even suicidal thoughts. Words, as Proverbs reminds us, *"have the power of life and death"* (Proverbs 18:21). When a spouse uses words to destroy rather than to build, the marriage ceases to reflect Christ's love and instead becomes a weapon of torment.

Many victims stay silent, believing their pain is invisible or insignificant. Yet the mental scars of verbal abuse run deep. A church that **fails to address** these realities honestly risks sending the message that image matters more than souls, and that silence is holier than truth.

Beyond "Staying for the Children"

Another damaging piece of advice often given is that a spouse should stay in an abusive marriage "for the sake of the kids." While children certainly need stability, they also need safety. A home filled with shouting, intimidation, and violence is **not a refuge**—it is a battlefield. Children raised in such environments often carry trauma into adulthood, repeating cycles of dysfunction in their own relationships. Protecting them sometimes means removing them from the very environment that is breaking them.

The church must exercise great caution here. Encouraging a victim to remain solely for the children's sake can inadvertently harm both the parent and the children. God does not call parents to martyr their **mental health** while their children absorb patterns of abuse. Instead, the call is to nurture, protect, and raise children in the fear of the Lord—something that is nearly impossible in a household governed by fear and rage.

A Call for Responsible Pastoral Care

Leaders must discern the difference between fighting for a marriage and binding someone to danger. To encourage reconciliation where repentance and transformation are absent is not pastoral wisdom; it is reckless counsel. Forgiveness may be extended, but trust and safety must be rebuilt through genuine repentance, accountability, and sometimes legal intervention. The church should be a place where victims **feel safe** to cry out, not a place where they are pressured into silence.

The body of Christ is called to protect the vulnerable, not preserve appearances. It is a holy responsibility to ensure that no one is coerced into remaining in **abuse** under the guise of faithfulness. Marriage is sacred, yes— but life is sacred too.

Restoring God's Vision for Marriage

God's vision for marriage is not tumult and torment, but peace and partnership. A Christ-centered union reflects love, respect, and safety. Anything else is a **counterfeit.** It is time for the church to repent where it has failed victims of marital abuse, to equip leaders with wisdom and compassion, and to model marriages that **truly honor** God.

When we silence abuse, we betray the gospel. But when we confront it, protect the hurting, and hold abusers accountable, we embody the heart of Christ—who came not to crush the weak, but to lift them up and give them life more abundantly.

Returning to God's Blueprint

The journey through these chapters has not been an easy one. We have confronted uncomfortable truths: manipulation masked as ministry, cult-like control within church walls, cliques and cancel culture that silence truth, racism that divides rather than unites, and the tragic enabling of abusive marriages. These are not light matters, but they must be addressed if the Church is to recover her true identity.

The truth is simple, yet sobering: what God established as His holy Bride has too often been corrupted by human agendas, personal ambition, and spiritual negligence. Church politics, secret societies, financial exploitation, favoritism, and silence in the face of sin have all contributed to the fractures we see today. Yet exposure is not meant for destruction. Exposure is meant for healing.

God has chosen me to declare the unfiltered truth of His Word. This assignment is not always easy, and it is not always welcomed. When God entrusts someone to be a bearer of truth, they must walk in boldness—unmoved by the fear of offense. Being a truth-bearer is not about chasing controversy; it is about standing as a witness to God's unchanging Word in love.

If our goal is to please people, we will constantly waver. When our desire is to please God, we will remain steadfast. Carnal church circles may pressure us to compromise, but platforms are temporary—eternal impact is what truly matters. My assignment is clear: I cannot deviate from doctrinal truth for the sake of acceptance. I do not want to hear, "Depart from me," while attempting to explain to Jesus that I stood with my name in lights, but never cried aloud.

The concerns highlighted in these volumes were not about bashing churches that build responsibly. This is about exposing wolves who profit and refuse to preach salvation, repentance for the backslider, and deliverance for the bound.

The Apostle Paul charged Timothy, saying: "Preach the word; be instant in season, out of season; reprove, rebuke, exhort with all longsuffering and doctrine." (2 Timothy 4:2)

Doors that seem promising may close. Jesus warned us: "And ye shall be hated of all men for my name's sake: but he that shall endure unto the end, the same shall be saved." (Mark 13:13)

We cannot afford to ignore these realities or sweep them under the rug in the name of "unity." Real unity is forged in truth, holiness, and repentance. A false peace that demands silence in the face of corruption is not peace at all—it is bondage. God is raising up a remnant who refuse to compromise, who will declare truth even when it is costly, and who love

Christ more than platforms, titles, or traditions.

My motive was not to condemn the Church, but to call her back to her blueprint: a sanctuary of holiness, a body marked by love, and a fellowship where Christ alone is glorified. It is a plea for leaders to repent where they have failed, for members to discern rather than blindly follow, and for all believers to choose consecration over religion.

The apostles did preach the Word, and part of preaching the Word is correcting error. Paul publicly named false teachers and rebuked them openly. He confronted Peter to his face when Peter was wrong (Galatians 2:11). He warned the church about Hymenaeus and Alexander (1 Timothy 1:19–20), and he named Hymenaeus and Philetus for spreading doctrine that corrupted the faith (2 Timothy 2:17). Titus was instructed to rebuke sharply those who subverted whole households (Titus 1:9–13).

Calling out error is not gossip, and it is not "preaching against people." It is shepherding. Silence in the face of doctrinal compromise is not love. Scripture commands leaders to contend for the faith once delivered (Jude 1:3) and to mark and avoid those who teach contrary to sound doctrine (Romans 16:17).

Jesus Himself publicly rebuked religious leaders for hypocrisy (Matthew 23). Truth has always been defended openly when error was public. Correction is not a distraction from the gospel—it is part of preaching Christ faithfully.

This work is not written from bitterness, jealousy, or a desire to harm reputations. It is written because the Church is too precious to be left unguarded, and because believers deserve truth **without mixture**. Where repentance is genuine, restoration is possible. Where deception is defended, exposure becomes necessary.

May the fear of the Lord return to the pulpit. May holiness return to leadership, and may the people of God be protected from wolves disguised as shepherds.

The good news is this: Jesus is still building His Church, and the gates of hell shall not prevail against it (Matthew 16:18). The systems of man will crumble, but the Kingdom of God will endure. If we return to prayer, holiness, accountability, and the unfiltered Word of God, the Church will not merely survive—she will shine as the spotless Bride Christ is coming back for.

The hour is urgent. The call is clear. The question remains: Will we repent, rebuild, and realign with God's design, or will we continue down the path of compromise? The choice is ours.

www.ingramcontent.com/pod-product-compliance
Lightning Source LLC
Chambersburg PA
CBHW032003080426
42735CB00007B/496